MW00768941

This book belongs to:

_____

24/7 CAFE

A Daily Sip
of Inspiration:
Volume 2

24/7 Cafe
A Daily Sip of Inspiration: Volume 2

Copyright © 2005 by FaithPoint Press

Produced by Cliff Road Books

ISBN: 1-58173-464-6

Book design by Pat Covert

Printed in China

24/7 CAFE

A Daily Sip of Inspiration: Volume 2

FaithP✦int™
PRESS

JANUARY 1

Morning: Today, you have 100% of your life left.
Tom Landry

Evening: The roots of true achievement lie in the will to become the best that you can become.
Harold Taylor

JANUARY 2

Morning: Happiness lies in the joy of achievement and the thrill of creative effort.
Franklin D. Roosevelt

Evening: Drop the idea that you are Atlas carrying the world on your shoulders. The world would go on even without you. Don't take yourself so seriously.
Norman Vincent Peale

JANUARY 3

Morning: Young people need models, not critics.
John Wooden

Evening: Our ambition should be to rule ourselves, the true kingdom for each one of us; and true progress is to know more, and be more, and to do more.
Sir John Lubbock

JANUARY 4

Morning: I believe in the imagination. What I cannot see is infinitely more important than what I can see.

Duane Michals

Evening: What you get by achieving your goals is not as important as what you become by achieving your goals.

Unknown

JANUARY 5

Morning: When you've got something to prove, there's nothing greater than a challenge.

Terry Bradshaw

Evening: I discovered I always have choices, and sometimes it's only a choice of attitude.

Judith M. Knowlton

JANUARY 6

Morning: There are only two ways to live your life. One is as though nothing is a miracle. The other is as if everything is.

Albert Einstein

Evening: What happens to a man is less significant than what happens within him.

Louis L. Mann

JANUARY 7

Morning: The world of achievement has always belonged to the optimist.

Harold Wilkins

Evening: There is more to life than increasing its speed.

Mahatma Gandhi

JANUARY 8

Morning: You will never be happy if you continue to search for what happiness consists of. You will never live if you are looking for the meaning of life.

Albert Camus

Evening: Take the attitude of a student: Never be too big to ask questions; never know too much to learn something new.

Og Mandino

JANUARY 9

Morning: It is not the position, but the disposition.

J. E. Dinger

Evening: We tend to live up to our expectations.

Earl Nightingale

JANUARY 10

Morning: It's how you deal with failure that determines how you achieve success.

David Feherty

Evening: Throw your heart over the fence and the rest will follow.

Norman Vincent Peale

JANUARY 11

Morning: Some say knowledge is power, but that is not true. Character is power.

Shri Sathya Sai Baba

Evening: Seldom does an individual exceed his own expectations.

Unknown

JANUARY 12

Morning: Youth is easily deceived, because it is quick to hope.

Aristotle

Evening: I never expect to lose. Even when I'm the underdog, I still prepare a victory speech.

H. Jackson Brown, Jr.

JANUARY 13

Morning: Pretend that every single person you meet has a sign around his or her neck that says, Make Me Feel Important. Not only will you succeed in sales, you will succeed in life.

Mary Kay Ash

Evening: Men take only their needs into consideration, never their abilities.

Napoleon Bonaparte

JANUARY 14

Morning: When your true purpose is to help others succeed, you succeed.

Unknown

Evening: A cloudy day is no match for a sunny disposition.

William Arthur Ward

JANUARY 15

Morning: An achievement is a bondage. It obliges one to a higher achievement.

Albert Camus

Evening: Big results require big ambitions.

James Champy

JANUARY 16

Morning: High expectations are the key to everything.

Sam Walton

Evening: Human beings can alter their lives by altering their attitudes.

Norman Vincent Peale

JANUARY 17

Morning: The difference between listening to a radio sermon and going to church ... is almost like the difference between calling your girl on the phone and spending an evening with her.

Dwight L. Moody

Evening: I take nothing for granted. I now have only good days or great days.

Lance Armstrong

JANUARY 18

Morning: Forget about all the reasons why something may not work. You only need to find one good reason why it will.

Robert Anthony

Evening: Live as you will have wished to have lived when you are dying.

Christian Furchtegott Gellert

JANUARY 19

Morning: Look well to this day. Yesterday is but a dream, and tomorrow is only a vision. But today well lived makes every yesterday a dream of happiness and every tomorrow a vision of hope. Look well therefore to this day.

Francis Gray

Evening: An optimist may see a light where there is none, but why must the pessimist always run to blow it out?

Michel De Saint-Pierre

JANUARY 20

Morning: We are all in the gutter, but some of us are looking at the stars.

Oscar Wilde

Evening: Nothing is good or bad, but thinking makes it so.

William Shakespeare

JANUARY 21

Morning: You have to stand for what you believe in. And sometimes you have to stand alone.

Queen Latifah

Evening: Let us, then, be up and doing, with a heart for any fate; still achieving, still pursuing, learn to labor and to wait.

Henry Wadsworth Longfellow

JANUARY 22

Morning: Act as though it is impossible to fail.
Unknown

Evening: There is no greater honor than to be the instrument in God's hands of leading one person out of the kingdom of Satan into the glorious light of Heaven.
Dwight L. Moody

JANUARY 23

Morning: Success doesn't make you, and failure doesn't break you.
Zig Ziglar

Evening: It is not because things are difficult that we do not dare; it is because we do not dare that they are difficult.
Seneca

JANUARY 24

Morning: Nothing can stop the man with the right mental attitude from achieving his goal; nothing on earth can help the man with the wrong mental attitude.
W. W. Ziege

Evening: No one has the right to hear the gospel twice, while there remains someone who has not heard it once.
Oswald J. Smith

JANUARY 25

Morning: Don't bother just to be better than your contemporaries or predecessors. Try to be better than yourself.

William Faulkner

Evening: Those who would make us feel must feel themselves.

Charles Churchill

JANUARY 26

Morning: The day the child realizes that all adults are imperfect, he becomes an adolescent; the day he forgives them, he becomes an adult; the day he forgives himself, he becomes wise.

Alden Nowlan

Evening: We grow neither better nor worse as we get old, but more like ourselves.

May Lamberton Becker

JANUARY 27

Morning: God speaks to us through our desires, then as we lay them at His feet, He helps us sort them out and quiets our hearts to accept what He has already prepared.

Rosalind Rinker

Evening: A champion hates to lose even more than she loves to win.

Chris Evert

JANUARY 28

Morning: I would rather make my name than inherit it.

W. M. Thackeray

Evening: Pessimism is not in being tired of evil but in being tired of good. Despair does not lie in being weary of suffering but in being weary of joy.

G. K. Chesterton

JANUARY 29

Morning: When all is said and done, the only thing you'll have left is your character.

Vince Gill

Evening: My father gave me the greatest gift anyone could give another person: He believed in me.

Jim Valvano

JANUARY 30

Morning: Do not regret growing old. It is a privilege denied to many.

Unknown

Evening: Our loyalties must transcend our race, our tribe, our class, and our nation, and this means we must develop a world perspective.

Martin Luther King, Jr.

JANUARY 31

Morning: Weakness of attitude becomes weakness of character.

Albert Einstein

Evening: Life's challenges are not supposed to paralyze you; they're supposed to help you discover who you are.

Bernice Johnson Reagon

FEBRUARY 1

Morning: The spirit, the will to win, and the will to excel are the things that endure. These qualities are so much more important than the events that occur.

Vincent Lombardi

Evening: The only way around is through.

Robert Frost

FEBRUARY 2

Morning: All things pass. Patience attains all it strives for.

Mother Teresa

Evening: He who fears being conquered is sure of defeat.

Napoleon

FEBRUARY 3

Morning: Enjoy life. This is not a dress rehearsal.

Unknown

Evening: No man is ever whipped, until he quits—in his own mind.

Napoleon Hill

FEBRUARY 4

Morning: Hate the sin, and love the sinner.

Mahatma Gandhi

Evening: You have to do what others won't to achieve what others don't.

Unknown

FEBRUARY 5

Morning: Life is a great big canvas, and you should throw all the paint you can on it.

Danny Kaye

Evening: Imagination is more important than knowledge. For knowledge is limited to all we now know and understand, while imagination embraces the entire world, and all there ever will be to know and understand.

Albert Einstein

FEBRUARY 6

Morning: If you don't like something, change it. If you can't change it, change your attitude. Don't complain.

Maya Angelou

Evening: The only thing that ever sat its way to success was a hen.

Sarah Brown

FEBRUARY 7

Morning: Rule number one: don't sweat the small stuff. Rule number two: it's all small stuff.

Robert Eliot

Evening: Today is the tomorrow we worried about yesterday.

Unknown

FEBRUARY 8

Morning: 99% of the failures come from people who have the habit of making excuses.

George Washington Carver

Evening: The man who removes a mountain begins by carrying away small stones.

Chinese Proverb

FEBRUARY 9

Morning: Nothing great will ever be achieved without great men, and men are great only if they are determined to be so.

Charles de Gaulle

Evening: I had ambition not only to go farther than any man had ever been before, but as far as it was possible for a man to go.

James R. Cook

FEBRUARY 10

Morning: The little troubles and worries of life may be as stumbling blocks in our way, or we may make them stepping-stones to a nobler character and to Heaven. Troubles are often the tools by which God fashions us for better things.

Henry Ward Beecher

Evening: Work for the fun of it, and the money will arrive some day.

Ronnie Milsap

FEBRUARY 11

Morning: Get action. Seize the moment. Man was never intended to become an oyster.

Theodore Roosevelt

Evening: Too much of a good thing is wonderful.

Mae West

FEBRUARY 12

Morning: History will be kind to me or I intend to write it.

Winston Churchill

Evening: I wash my hands of those who imagine chattering to be knowledge, silence to be ignorance, and affection to be art.

Kahlil Gibran

FEBRUARY 13

Morning: We must want for others, not ourselves alone.

Eleanor Roosevelt

Evening: I keep my ideals, because in spite of everything, I still believe that people are really good at heart.

Anne Frank

FEBRUARY 14

Morning: Life is not so short but that there is always time for courtesy.

Ralph Waldo Emerson

Evening: Children need love, especially when they don't deserve it.

Unknown

FEBRUARY 15

Morning: The toughest thing about success is that you've got to keep on being a success.

Irving Berlin

Evening: Courage is resistance to fear, mastery of fear—not absence of fear. Except a creature be part coward, it is not a compliment to say it is brave.

Mark Twain

FEBRUARY 16

Morning: The men who succeed are the efficient few. They are the few who have the ambition and will power to develop themselves.

Herbert N. Casson

Evening: What the caterpillar calls the end, the rest of the world calls a butterfly.

Lao Tzu

FEBRUARY 17

Morning: He who is devoid of the power to forgive, is devoid of the power to love.

Martin Luther King, Jr.

Evening: I had no ambition to make a fortune. Mere money-making has never been my goal. I had an ambition to build.

John D. Rockefeller

FEBRUARY 18

Morning: Attitudes are more important than facts.

Karl A. Menninger

Evening: Imagination disposes of everything; it creates beauty, justice, and happiness, which are everything in this world.

Blaise Pascal

FEBRUARY 19

Morning: Dream as if you'll live forever. Live as if you'll die today.

James Dean

Evening: Those who are not looking for happiness are the most likely to find it, because those who are searching forget that the surest way to be happy is to seek happiness for others.

Martin Luther King, Jr.

FEBRUARY 20

Morning: Enter every activity without giving mental recognition to the possibility of defeat. Concentrate on your strengths instead of your weaknesses, on your powers instead of your problems.

Paul J. Meyer

Evening: It doesn't matter if you win or lose—until you lose.

Unknown

FEBRUARY 21

Morning: Life is a series of experiences, each one of which makes us bigger, even though sometimes it is hard to realize this.

Henry Ford

Evening: Life without liberty is like a body without spirit.

Kahlil Gibran

FEBRUARY 22

Morning: An inexhaustible good nature is one of the most precious gifts of heaven, spreading itself like oil over the troubled sea of thought, and keeping the mind smooth and equable in the roughest weather.

Washington Irving

Evening: We're fools whether we dance or not, so we might as well dance.

Japanese Proverb

FEBRUARY 23

Morning: Life is the only game in which the object of the game is to learn the rules.

Ashleigh Brilliant

Evening: People who never achieve happiness are the ones who complain whenever they're awake, and whenever they're asleep, they're thinking about what to complain about tomorrow.

Adam Zimbler

FEBRUARY 24

Morning: Adventure isn't hanging on a rope off the side of a mountain. Adventure is an attitude that we must apply to the day-to-day obstacles of life—facing new challenges, seizing new opportunities, testing our resources against the unknown, and in the process, discovering our own unique potential.

John Amatt

Evening: For success, attitude is equally as important as ability.

Harry F. Banks

FEBRUARY 25

Morning: We choose our joys and sorrows long before we experience them.

Kahlil Gibran

Evening: The greatest strength is gentleness.

Iroquois Proverb

FEBRUARY 26

Morning: A constant struggle, a ceaseless battle to bring success from inhospitable surroundings, is the price of all great achievements.

Orison Swett Marden

Evening: Live life today. Yesterday is gone, and tomorrow may never come.

Unknown

FEBRUARY 27

Morning: My attitude is never to be satisfied, never enough, never.

Bela Karolyi

Evening: I love living. I have some problems with my life, but living is the best thing they've come up with so far.

Neil Simon

FEBRUARY 28

Morning: You know, by the time you reach my age, you've made plenty of mistakes if you've lived your life properly.

Ronald Reagan

Evening: It's your aptitude, not just your attitude, that determines your ultimate altitude.

Zig Ziglar

FEBRUARY 29

Morning: The hardest thing in life is to know which bridge to cross and which to burn.

David Russell

Evening: Without ambition one starts nothing. Without work one finishes nothing. The prize will not be sent to you. You have to win it.

Ralph Waldo Emerson

MARCH 1

Morning: Great spirits have always encountered violent opposition from mediocre minds.

Albert Einstein

Evening: The greatest discovery of my gene ration is that a man can alter his life simply by altering his attitude of mind.

William James

MARCH 2

Morning: Smile. It increases your face value.

Dolly Parton

Evening: I have the simplest tastes. I am always satisfied with the best.

Oscar Wilde

MARCH 3

Morning: Life is like a piano. What you get out of it depends on how you play it.

Unknown

Evening: The greatest part of our happiness depends on our dispositions, not our circumstances.

Martha Washington

MARCH 4

Morning: Always bear in mind that your own resolution to succeed is more important than any other one thing.

Abraham Lincoln

Evening: Happiness is not a goal; it is a by-product.

Eleanor Roosevelt

MARCH 5

Morning: We can easily manage if we will only take, each day, the burden appointed to it. But the load will be too heavy for us if we carry yesterday's burden over again today, and then add the burden of the morrow before we are required to bear it.

John Newton

Evening: Big shots are only little shots who keep shooting.

Christopher Morley

MARCH 6

Morning: Almost always, the creative dedicated minority has made the world better.

Martin Luther King, Jr.

Evening: Men can only be happy when they do not assume that the object of life is happiness.

George Orwell

MARCH 7

Morning: A happy person is not a person in a certain set of circumstances, but rather a person with a certain set of attitudes.

Hugh Downs

Evening: Always look at what you have left. Never look at what you have lost.

Robert Schuller

MARCH 8

Morning: When you're a winner, you're always happy, but if you're happy as a loser, you'll always be a loser.

Mark Fidrych

Evening: A pessimist sees only the dark side of the clouds, and mopes; a philosopher sees both sides, and shrugs; an optimist doesn't see the clouds at all—he's walking on them.

Leonard Louis Levinson

MARCH 9

Morning: Excellence is not a skill. It is an attitude.

Ralph Marston

Evening: An optimist is a person who sees a green light everywhere, while a pessimist sees only the red stoplight. The truly wise person is colorblind.

Albert Schweitzer

MARCH 10

Morning: Only those who dare to fail greatly can ever achieve greatly.

Robert Kennedy

Evening: We make way for the man who boldly pushes past us.

Christian Nevell Bovee

MARCH 11

Morning: It's not what happens to you, but how you react to it that matters.

Epictetus

Evening: One day at a time—this is enough. Do not look back and grieve over the past for it is gone; and do not be troubled about the future, for it has not yet come. Live in the present, and make it so beautiful that it will be worth remembering.

Unknown

MARCH 12

Morning: Logic will get you from A to B. Imagination will take you everywhere.

Albert Einstein

Evening: If I have seen farther than others, it is because I have stood on the shoulders of giants.

Sir Isaac Newton

MARCH 13

Morning: Youth is the gift of nature, but age is a work of art.
Stanislaw Jerzy Lec

Evening: Your aspirations are your possibilities.
Samuel Johnson

MARCH 14

Morning: The whole being of any Christian is faith and love. Faith brings the man to God; love brings him to men.
Martin Luther

Evening: Our business in life is not to succeed, but to continue to fail in good spirits.
Robert Louis Stevenson

MARCH 15

Morning: Our imagination is the only limit to what we can hope to have in the future.
Charles Kettering

Evening: If you have a great ambition, take as big a step as possible in the direction of fulfilling it. The step may only be a tiny one, but trust that it may be the largest one possible for now.
Mildred Mcafee

MARCH 16

Morning: One characteristic of winners is that they always look upon themselves as a do-it-yourself project.

Denis Waitley

Evening: It's not the load that breaks you down; it's the way you carry it.

Lena Horne

MARCH 17

Morning: A healthy attitude is contagious, but don't wait to catch it from others. Be a carrier.

Unknown

Evening: Toughness is in the soul and spirit, not in muscles.

Alex Karras

MARCH 18

Morning: If you aren't fired with enthusiasm, you will be fired with enthusiasm.

Vincent Lombardi

Evening: Keep a green tree in your heart and perhaps a singing bird will come.

Chinese Proverb

MARCH 19

Morning: Attitude is a little thing that makes a big difference.

Winston Churchill

Evening: If I have the belief that I can do it, I shall surely acquire the capacity to do it even if I may not have it at the beginning.

Mahatma Gandhi

MARCH 20

Morning: God sends trials to strengthen our trust in him so that our faith will not fail. Our trials keep us trusting; they burn away our self confidence and drive us to our Saviour.

Edmund Clowney

Evening: His authority on earth allows us to dare to go to all the nations. His authority in heaven gives us our only hope of success. And His presence with us leaves us no other choice.

John R. W. Stott

MARCH 21

Morning: People who are unable to motivate themselves must be content with mediocrity, no matter how impressive their other talents.

Andrew Carnegie

Evening: Tough times never last, but tough people do.

Robert Schuller

MARCH 22

Morning: I really don't think life is about the
I-could-have-beens. Life is only about the
I-tried-to-do. I don't mind the failure, but I can't
imagine that I'd forgive myself if I didn't try.
Nikki Giovanni

Evening: Men who never get carried away
should be.

Malcolm Forbes

MARCH 23

Morning: Anybody can do just about anything
with himself that he really wants to and makes
up his mind to do. We are capable of greater
things than we realize.

Norman Vincent Peale

Evening: A person will sometimes devote all
his life to the development of one part of his
body—the wishbone.

Robert Frost

MARCH 24

Morning: Things turn out best for the people
who make the best out of the way things turn
out.

Art Linkletter

Evening: We cannot direct the wind, but we
can adjust the sails.

Unknown

MARCH 25

Morning: The only disability in life is a bad attitude.

Scott Hamilton

Evening: Never worry about numbers. Help one person at a time, and always start with the person nearest you.

Mother Teresa

MARCH 26

Morning: If you don't think every day is a good day, just try missing one.

Cavett Robert

Evening: There is nothing so fatal to character as half-finished tasks.

David Lloyd George

MARCH 27

Morning: The achievements which society rewards are won at the cost of diminution of personality.

Carl Jung

Evening: We should be too big to take offense and too noble to give it.

Abraham Lincoln

MARCH 28

Morning: When God comes down, He removes the immovable difficulties. When God comes down, the impossible becomes reality.

Unknown

Evening: It is better to light one small candle than to curse the darkness.

Confucius

MARCH 29

Morning: Cheerfulness and contentment are great beautifiers and are famous preservers of youthful looks.

Charles Dickens

Evening: Always show the you in you that makes you the you that you are.

Chidinma Obietikponah

MARCH 30

Morning: We must not, in trying to think about how we can make a big difference, ignore the small daily differences we can make which, over time, add up to big differences that we often cannot foresee.

Marian Wright Edelman

Evening: Share our similarities; celebrate our differences.

M. Scott Peck

MARCH 31

Morning: An inordinate passion for pleasure is the secret of remaining young.
Oscar Wilde

Evening: Change yourself, and your work will seem different.
Norman Vincent Peale

APRIL 1

Morning: Change your thoughts, and you change your world.
Norman Vincent Peale

Evening: Great things are not done by impulse, but by a series of small things brought together.
Vincent Van Gogh

APRIL 2

Morning: What makes life worth living is knowing that one day you'll wake up and find the person that makes you happier than anything in the whole world. So don't ever lose hope and give up. Everything turns out okay, and the good guy always wins.
Unknown

Evening: Darkness cannot drive out darkness; only light can do that. Hate cannot drive out hate; only love can do that.
Martin Luther King, Jr.

APRIL 3

Morning: Be daring, be different, be impractical, be anything that will assert integrity of purpose and imaginative vision against the play-it-safers, the creatures of the commonplace, the slaves of the ordinary.

Cecil Beaton

Evening: We boil at different degrees.

Ralph Waldo Emerson

APRIL 4

Morning: There is something that is much more scarce, something rarer than ability. It is the ability to recognize ability.

Robert Half

Evening: In order to be irreplaceable, one must always be different.

Coco Chanel

APRIL 5

Morning: If you want to stand out, don't be different; be outstanding.

Meredith West

Evening: If there are things you don't like in the world you grew up in, make your own life different.

Dave Thomas

APRIL 6

Morning: Achievement is largely the product of steadily raising one's levels of aspiration ... and expectation.

Jack Nicklaus

Evening: Most of our obstacles would melt away if, instead of cowering before them, we should make up our minds to walk boldly through them.

Orison Swett Marden

APRIL 7

Morning: The hardest struggle of all is to be something different from what the average man is.

Charles M. Schwab

Evening: When we lose the right to be different, we lose the privilege to be free.

Charles Evans Hughes

APRIL 8

Morning: He who is not every day conquering some fear has not learned the secret of life.

Ralph Waldo Emerson

Evening: Each player must accept the cards life deals him or her: but once they are in hand, he or she alone must decide how to play the cards in order to win the game.

Voltaire

APRIL 9

Morning: If you do things well, do them better. Be daring, be first, be different, be just.

Anita Roddick

Evening: Every individual in an organization is motivated by something different.

Rick Pitino

APRIL 10

Morning: Formulate and stamp indelibly on your mind a mental picture of yourself as succeeding. Hold this picture tenaciously. Never permit it to fade. Your mind will seek to develop the picture. Do not build up obstacles in your imagination.

Norman Vincent Peale

Evening: A person who aims at nothing is sure to hit it.

Unknown

APRIL 11

Morning: Plunge boldly into the thick of life, and seize it where you will. It is always interesting.

Johann Wolfgang von Goethe

Evening: A man ought to live so that everybody knows he is a Christian ... and most of all, his family ought to know.

Dwight L. Moody

APRIL 12

Morning: Of all human activities, man's listening to God is the supreme act of his reasoning and will.

Pope Paul VI

Evening: A grownup is a child with layers on.

Woody Harrelson

APRIL 13

Morning: Be bold, be bold, and everywhere be bold.

Herbert Spencer

Evening: Live daringly, boldly, fearlessly. Taste the relish to be found in competition—in having put forth the best within you.

Henry J. Kaiser

APRIL 14

Morning: Anyone can sing in the sunshine. It takes people of true courage and fortitude to be able to sing in the rain.

Marian Wright Edelman

Evening: There are no great people in this world, only great challenges which ordinary people rise to meet.

William Frederick Halsey, Jr.

APRIL 15

Morning: Imagination is everything. It is the preview of life's coming attractions.
Albert Einstein

Evening: The meaning of life is to give life meaning.
Unknown

APRIL 16

Morning: That old law about "an eye for an eye" leaves everybody blind. The time is always right to do the right thing.
Martin Luther King, Jr.

Evening: Never do things others can do and will do if there are things others cannot do or will not do.
Amelia Earhart

APRIL 17

Morning: Never leave that 'till tomorrow which you can do today.
Benjamin Franklin

Evening: Finish each day and be done with it. You have done what you could. Some blunders and absurdities no doubt crept in; forget them as soon as you can. Tomorrow is a new day; begin it well and serenely and with too high a spirit to be encumbered with your old nonsense.
Ralph Waldo Emerson

APRIL 18

Morning: Success is not final; failure is not fatal. It is the courage to continue that counts.
Winston Churchill

Evening: Faith crosses every border and touches every heart in every nation.
George W. Bush

APRIL 19

Morning: Challenges are what make life interesting; overcoming them is what makes life meaningful.
Joshua J. Marine

Evening: I have little patience with scientists who take a board of wood, look for its thinnest part, and drill a great number of holes where drilling is easy.
Albert Einstein

APRIL 20

Morning: The man who does things makes many mistakes, but he never makes the biggest mistake of all—doing nothing.
Benjamin Franklin

Evening: You must play boldly to win.
Arnold Palmer

APRIL 21

Morning: The reward of a thing well done is to have done it.

Ralph Waldo Emerson

Evening: The best way to predict your future is to create it.

Unknown

APRIL 22

Morning: The greatest glory in living lies not in never falling, but in rising every time we fall.

Nelson Mandella

Evening: If you rest, you rust.

Helen Keller

APRIL 23

Morning: I have not failed. I've just found 10,000 ways that won't work.

Thomas Edison

Evening: The saints are the sinners who keep going.

Robert Louis Stevenson

APRIL 24

Morning: Man's only true happiness is to live in hope of something to be won by him. Reverence something to be worshipped by him, and love something to be cherished by him, forever.

John Ruskin

Evening: It's not that I'm so smart; it's just that I stay with problems longer.

Albert Einstein

APRIL 25

Morning: The average man does not know what to do with this life, yet wants another one which will last forever.

Anatole France

Evening: Greatness does not approach him who is forever looking down.

Hitopadesa

APRIL 26

Morning: If you wish your merit to be known, acknowledge that of other people.

Asian Proverb

Evening: He who loses himself in passion has lost less than he who loses his passion.

St. Augustine

APRIL 27

Morning: Lord, remove every barrier the enemy has put in place, so that the only barrier which remains is the cross itself.

Jon Reid

Evening: It's easy to follow when we want to go where the leader is taking us, but what about when He takes a turn we're not in favor of?

Lisa Barry

APRIL 28

Morning: Don't worry about life; you're not going to survive it anyway.

Unknown

Evening: An individual has not started living until he can rise above the narrow confines of his individualistic concerns to the broader concerns of all humanity.

Martin Luther King, Jr.

APRIL 29

Morning: Through perseverance many people win success out of what seemed destined to be certain failure.

Benjamin Disraeli

Evening: If it seems a childish thing to do, do it in remembrance that you are a child.

Frederick Buechner

APRIL 30

Morning: A man is what he thinks about all day long.

Ralph Waldo Emerson

Evening: Little minds attain and are subdued by misfortunes, but great minds rise above them.

Washington Irving

MAY 1

Morning: Having once decided to achieve a certain task, achieve it at all costs of tedium and distaste. The gain in self confidence of having accomplished a tiresome labor is immense.

Thomas A. Bennett

Evening: Every action of our lives touches on some chord that will vibrate in eternity.

E. Chapin

MAY 2

Morning: What seems impossible one minute becomes, through faith, possible the next.

Norman Vincent Peale

Evening: Give me a lever long enough and a prop strong enough. I can single-handedly move the world.

Archimedes

MAY 3

Morning: Do not say, "It is morning," and dismiss it with a name of yesterday. See it for the first time as a newborn child that has no name.
Rabindranath Tagore

Evening: The future of civilization depends on our overcoming the meaninglessness and hopelessness that characterizes the thoughts of men today.
Albert Schweitzer

MAY 4

Morning: The mind is its own place, and in itself, can make heaven of Hell, and a hell of Heaven.
John Milton

Evening: Aerodynamically, the bumblebee shouldn't be able to fly, but the bumblebee doesn't know it, so it goes on flying anyway.
Mary Kay Ash

MAY 5

Morning: If you put a small value on yourself, rest assured that the world will not raise your price.
Unknown

Evening: One of the redeeming things about being an athlete is redefining what is humanly possible.
Lance Armstrong

MAY 6

Morning: Life is too important to be taken seriously.

Oscar Wilde

Evening: There are no rules here—we're trying to accomplish something.

Thomas Edison

MAY 7

Morning: A positive attitude can really make dreams come true—it did for me.

Zina Garrison

Evening: Faith is believing He, the miracle worker, can turn my stone-cold indifference into a fire of love toward certain "unlovables."

Pamela Reeve

MAY 8

Morning: Life's problems wouldn't be called "hurdles" if there wasn't a way to get over them.

Unknown

Evening: We are at our very best, and we are happiest, when we are fully engaged in work we enjoy on the journey toward the goal we've established for ourselves. It gives meaning to our time off and comfort to our sleep. It makes everything else in life so wonderful, so worthwhile.

Earl Nightingale

MAY 9

Morning: The brain is like muscle. When we think well, we feel good. Understanding is a kind of ecstasy.

Carl Sagan

Evening: Don't ask yourself what the world needs; ask yourself what makes you come alive. And then go and do that. Because what the world needs is people who have come alive.

Harold Whitman

MAY 10

Morning: A difficult time can be more readily endured if we retain the conviction that our existence holds a purpose—a cause to pursue, a person to love, a goal to achieve.

John Maxwell

Evening: Life without a friend is like death without a witness.

Spanish Proverb

MAY 11

Morning: Home run hitters strike out a lot.

Reggie Jackson

Evening: It doesn't matter how many say it cannot be done or how many people have tried it before; it's important to realize that whatever you're doing, it's your first attempt at it.

Wally Amos

MAY 12

Morning: The innovation point is the pivotal moment when talented and motivated people seek the opportunity to act on their ideas and dreams.

W. Arthur Porter

Evening: Prayer does not mean asking God for all kinds of things we want; it is rather the desire for God Himself, the only Giver of Life.

Sadhu Sundar Singh

MAY 13

Morning: Your work is to discover your work and then with all your heart to give yourself to it.

Buddha

Evening: Only he who can say, "The Lord is the strength of my life," can say, "Of whom shall I be afraid?"

Alexander MacLaren

MAY 14

Morning: When you turn your heart and your life over to Christ, when you accept Christ as the savior, it changes your heart.

George W. Bush

Evening: No bird soars too high, if he soars with his own wings.

William Blake

MAY 15

Morning: Always do what you are afraid to do.

Ralph Waldo Emerson

Evening: The purpose of man is in action not thought.

Thomas Carlyle

MAY 16

Morning: Many persons have a wrong idea of what constitutes true happiness. It is not attained through self gratification but through fidelity to a worthy purpose.

Helen Keller

Evening: On the mountains of truth you can never climb in vain: Either you will reach a point higher up today, or you will be training your powers, so that you will be able to climb higher tomorrow.

Friedrich Nietzsche

MAY 17

Morning: The measure of success is not whether you have a tough problem to deal with, but whether it is the same problem you had last year.

John Foster Dulles

Evening: Men try to fix problems with duct tape. God did it with nails.

Unknown

MAY 18

Morning: The best things in life come in threes, like friends, dreams, and memories.

Unknown

Evening: Six essential qualities are the key to success: sincerity, personal integrity, humility, courtesy, wisdom, charity.

William Menninger

MAY 19

Morning: Someone's opinion of you does not have to become your reality.

Les Brown

Evening: Speak when you are angry, and you will make the best speech you will ever regret.

Ambrose Bierce

MAY 20

Morning: The sports page records people's accomplishments; the front page usually records nothing but man's failures.

Earl Warren

Evening: If God were small enough to be understood, He would not be big enough to be worshiped.

Evelyn Underhill

MAY 21

Morning: When you have a number of disagreeable duties to perform, always do the most disagreeable first.

Josiah Quincy

Evening: He who governed the world before I was born shall take care of it likewise when I am dead. My part is to improve the present moment.

John Wesley

MAY 22

Morning: To the wise, life is a problem; to the fool, a solution.

Marcus Aurelius Antoninus

Evening: Trust the past to God's mercy, the present to God's love, and the future to God's providence.

St. Augustine

MAY 23

Morning: Those who wish to sing always find a song.

Swedish Proverb

Evening: The way I see it, if you want the rainbow, you gotta put up with the rain.

Dolly Parton

MAY 24

Morning: This is my life. It is my one time to be me. I want to experience every good thing.
Maya Angelou

Evening: We must alter our lives in order to alter our hearts, for it is impossible to live one way and pray another.
William Law

MAY 25

Morning: One who condones evils is just as guilty as the one who perpetrates it.
Martin Luther King, Jr.

Evening: Life was meant to be lived, and curiosity must be kept alive. One must never, for whatever reason, turn his back on life.
Eleanor Roosevelt

MAY 26

Morning: The point of power is always in the present moment.
Louise L. Hay

Evening: Our attitude toward life determines life's attitude toward us.
Earl Nightingale

MAY 27

Morning: Look at life through the windshield, not the rear-view mirror.

Byrd Baggett

Evening: God gives us dreams a size too big so that we can grow into them.

Unknown

MAY 28

Morning: The person born with a talent they are meant to use will find their greatest happiness in using it.

Johann Wolfgang von Goethe

Evening: You have powers you never dreamed of. You can do things you never thought you could do. There are no limitations in what you can do except the limitations of your own mind.

Darwin P. Kingsley

MAY 29

Morning: When I hear somebody sigh, "Life is hard," I am always tempted to ask, "Compared to what?"

Sydney J. Harris

Evening: You don't develop courage by being happy in your relationships everyday. You develop it by surviving difficult times and challenging adversity.

Barbara De Angelis

MAY 30

Morning: Love is stronger than death even though it can't stop death from happening, but no matter how hard death tries, it can't separate people from love. It can't take away our memories either. In the end, life is stronger than death.

Unknown

Evening: No one is useless in this world who lightens the burdens of another.

Charles Dickens

MAY 31

Morning: You are only as strong as your purpose, therefore let us choose reasons to act that are big, bold, righteous, and eternal.

Barry Munro

Evening: Good luck is another name for tenacity of purpose.

Ralph Waldo Emerson

JUNE 1

Morning: If we don't change, we don't grow. If we don't grow, we aren't really living.

Gail Sheehy

Evening: If you view all the things that happen to you, both good and bad, as opportunities, then you operate out of a higher level of consciousness.

Les Brown

JUNE 2

Morning: Like what you do. If you don't like it, do something else.

Paul Harvey

Evening: When thou prayest, rather let thy heart be without words than thy words be without heart.

John Bunyan

JUNE 3

Morning: Each person's only hope for improving his lot rests on his recognizing the true nature of his basic personality, surrendering to it, and becoming who he is.

Sheldon Kopp

Evening: It is one of the most beautiful compensations of life, that no man can sincerely try to help another without helping himself.

Lao Tzu

JUNE 4

Morning: The times we find ourselves having to wait on others may be the perfect opportunities to train ourselves to wait on the Lord.

Joni Eareckson Tada

Evening: Love is a great beautifier.

Louisa May Alcott

JUNE 5

Morning: In the middle of difficulty lies opportunity.

Albert Einstein

Evening: Faith attracts the positive. Fear attracts the negative.

Ed Cole

JUNE 6

Morning: You are never given a wish without also being given the power to make it come true. You may have to work for it, however.

Richard Bach

Evening: Don't waste your youth growing up.

Unknown

JUNE 7

Morning: We make a living by what we get, but we make a life by what we give.

Winston Churchill

Evening: You must understand the whole of life, not just one little part of it. That is why you must read, that is why you must look at the skies, that is why you must sing and dance, and write poems, and suffer, and understand, for all that is life.

J. Krishnamurti

JUNE 8

Morning: Life is too short to be little. Man is never so manly as when he feels deeply, acts boldly, and expresses himself with frankness and with fervor.

Benjamin Disraeli

Evening: Life's a voyage that's homeward bound.

Herman Melville

JUNE 9

Morning: Life is to be lived. If you have to support yourself, you had bloody well better find some way that is going to be interesting.

Katharine Hepburn

Evening: No legacy is so rich as honesty.

William Shakespeare

JUNE 10

Morning: Whether it's the best of times or the worst of times, it's the only time we've got.

Art Buchwald

Evening: Whence comes this idea that if what we are doing is fun, it can't be God's will? The God who made giraffes, a baby's fingernails, a puppy's tail, a crooknecked squash, the bobwhite's call, and a young girl's giggle has a sense of humor. Make no mistake about that.

Catherine Marshall

JUNE 11

Morning: Great minds have purposes, little minds have wishes.

Washington Irving

Evening: There are two ways of spreading light—to be the candle or the mirror that reflects it.

Edith Wharton

JUNE 12

Morning: For what is the best choice, for each individual is the highest it is possible for him to achieve.

Aristotle

Evening: Our truest life is when we are in dreams awake.

Henry David Thoreau

JUNE 13

Morning: Wisdom is the power to see and the inclination to choose the best and highest goal, together with the surest means of attaining it.

James Packer

Evening: Reflect on your present blessings, of which every man has many, and not on your past misfortunes, of which all men have some.

Charles Dickens

JUNE 14

Morning: Taken separately, the experiences of life can work harm and not good. Taken together, they make a pattern of blessing and strength the like of which the world does not know.

V. Raymond Brown

Evening: When I see beauty in myself, that's when I am beautiful to others.

Unknown

JUNE 15

Morning: You can come to understand your purpose in life by slowing down and feeling your heart's desires.

Marcia Wieder

Evening: However young, the seeker who sets out upon the way shines brightly over the world.

Buddha

JUNE 16

Morning: God gives us each a song.

Ute Proverb

Evening: If the first woman God ever made was strong enough to turn the world upside down all alone, these women together ought to be able to turn it back and get it right side up again!

Sojourner Truth

JUNE 17

Morning: Make your work to be in keeping with your purpose.

Leonardo da Vinci

Evening: Ambition is the germ from which all growth of nobleness proceeds.

Thomas Dunn English

JUNE 18

Morning: No one can make you feel inferior without your consent.

Eleanor Roosevelt

Evening: Friends are the family we choose for ourselves.

Edna Buchanan

JUNE 19

Morning: What mankind wants is not talent; it is purpose.

Edward G. Bulwer-Lytton

Evening: Wherever you are, it is your friends who make the world.

William James

JUNE 20

Morning: A friend is one to whom one may pour out all the contents of one's heart, chaff and grain together, knowing that the gentlest of hands will take and sift it, keep what is worth keeping, and with a breath of kindness blow the rest away.

Arabic Proverb

Evening: Believe your dreams—they are wiser than we are.

Unknown

JUNE 21

Morning: Where your talents and the needs of the world cross lies your calling.

Aristotle

Evening: The best is yet to be.

Robert Browning

JUNE 22

Morning: What would life be if we had no courage to attempt anything?

Vincent van Gogh

Evening: Peace is always beautiful.

Walt Whitman

JUNE 23

Morning: Love what you do. Do what you love.

Wayne Dyer

Evening: You already possess everything you need to be great.

Crow Proverb

JUNE 24

Morning: Nothing splendid has ever been achieved except by those who dared believe that something inside them was superior to circumstances.

Bruce Barton

Evening: I am a woman above everything else.

Jacqueline Kennedy Onassis

JUNE 25

Morning: Be careful of what you set your heart on, for it will surely be yours.

Ralph Waldo Emerson

Evening: The way to love anything is to realize that it might be lost.

G. K. Chesterton

JUNE 26

Morning: Life without love is a shadow of things that might be.

Unknown

Evening: When men and women are able to respect and accept their differences, then love has a chance to blossom.

John Gray

JUNE 27

Morning: The first thing is to love your sport. Never do it to please someone else. It has to be yours.

Peggy Fleming

Evening: Look within. Be still. Free from fear and attachment, know the sweet joy of the way.

Buddha

JUNE 28

Morning: Do not wait for leaders. Do it alone, person to person.

Mother Teresa

Evening: The word of God hidden in the heart is a stubborn voice to suppress.

Billy Graham

JUNE 29

Morning: Whatever you vividly imagine, ardently desire, sincerely believe, and enthusiastically act upon ... must inevitably come to pass.

Paul Meyer

Evening: True friendship can afford true knowledge. It does not depend on darkness and ignorance.

Henry David Thoreau

JUNE 30

Morning: Life is inherently risky. There is only one big risk you should avoid at all costs, and that is the risk of doing nothing.

Denis Waitley

Evening: Ambition never comes to an end.

Yoshida Kenko

JULY 1

Morning: Nobody can be successful if he doesn't love his work, love his job.

David Sarnoff

Evening: A peacock who sits on her tailfeathers is just another turkey.

Unknown

JULY 2

Morning: Like the moon, come out from behind the clouds! Shine.

Buddha

Evening: Have a heart that never hardens, a temper that never tires, a touch that never hurts.

Charles Dickens

JULY 3

Morning: We tend to defend vigorously things that in our deepest hearts we are not quite certain about. If we are certain of something we know, it doesn't need defending.

Madeleine L'Engle

Evening: A woman is like a tea bag. You never know how strong she is until she gets into hot water.

Eleanor Roosevelt

JULY 4

Morning: Become so wrapped up in something that you forget to be afraid.

Lady Bird Johnson

Evening: To place ourselves in range of God's choicest gifts, we have to walk with God, work with God, lean on God, cling to God, come to have the sense and feel of God, refer all things to God.

Cornelius Plantinga, Jr.

JULY 5

Morning: Be not simply good; be good for something.

Henry David Thoreau

Evening: Nothing is a waste of time if you use the experience wisely.

Auguste Rodin

JULY 6

Morning: Time goes by so fast; people go in and out of your life. You must never miss the opportunity to tell these people how much they mean to you.

Unknown

Evening: If what you're working for really matters, you'll give it all you've got.

Nido Qubein

JULY 7

Morning: A great pleasure in life is doing what people say you cannot do.

Walter Bagehot

Evening: You can make more friends in two months by becoming interested in other people than you can in two years by trying to get other people interested in you.

Dale Carnegie

JULY 8

Morning: When written in Chinese, the word crisis is composed of two characters. One represents danger, and the other represents opportunity.

John F. Kennedy

Evening: God turns the ordinary into the extraordinary.

Erwin Tippel

JULY 9

Morning: Believe it is possible to solve your problem. Tremendous things happen to the believer. So believe the answer will come. It will.

Norman Vincent Peale

Evening: I am always doing things I can't do; that's how I get to do them.

Pablo Picasso

JULY 10

Morning: Be bold. If you are going to make an error, make a doozy, and don't be afraid to hit the ball.

Billie Jean King

Evening: The happiness of your life depends upon the quality of your thoughts. Take care that you entertain no notions unsuitable to virtue and reasonable nature.

Marcus Aurelius Antoninus

JULY 11

Morning: Hope is patiently waiting expectantly for the intangible to become reality.

Avery D. Miller

Evening: It's not hard to make decisions when you know what your values are.

Roy Disney

JULY 12

Morning: It is better to conquer yourself than to win a thousand battles. Then the victory is yours. It cannot be taken from you, not by angels or by demons, heaven or hell.

Buddha

Evening: This year, or this month, or, more likely, this very day, we have failed to practice ourselves the kind of behavior we expect from other people.

C. S. Lewis

JULY 13

Morning: Always remember to slow down in life; live, breathe, and learn; take a look around you whenever you have time and never forget everything and every person that has the least place within your heart.

Unknown

Evening: Wheresoever you go, go with all your heart.

Confucius

JULY 14

Morning: It seems to me that trying to live without friends is like milking a bear to get cream for your morning coffee. It is a whole lot of trouble, and then not worth much after you get it.
Zorah Neale Hurston

Evening: Failures are finger posts on the road to achievement.
Charles Kettering

JULY 15

Morning: Always be a first-rate version of yourself, instead of a second-rate version of somebody else.
Judy Garland

Evening: Faith is not a storm cellar to which men and women can flee for refuge from the storms of life. It is, instead, an inner force that gives them the strength to face those storms and their consequences with serenity of spirit.
Sam J. Ervin, Jr.

JULY 16

Morning: The greatest thing about man is his ability to transcend himself, his ancestry, and his environment and to become what he dreams of being.
Tully C. Knoles

Evening: A word of kindness can warm three winter months.
Japanese Proverb

JULY 17

Morning: A life spent making mistakes is not only more honorable but more useful than a life spent doing nothing.

George Bernard Shaw

Evening: Kindness and honesty can only be expected from the strong.

Unknown

JULY 18

Morning: Knowing others is intelligence; knowing yourself is true wisdom. Mastering others is strength; mastering yourself is true power.

Lao Tzu

Evening: He who would learn to fly one day must first learn to stand and walk and run and climb and dance; one cannot fly into flying.

Friedrich Nietzsche

JULY 19

Morning: Positive thinking won't let you do anything, but it will let you do everything better than negative thinking will.

Zig Ziglar

Evening: Responsibility is the thing people dread most of all. Yet it is the one thing in the world that develops us, gives us manhood or womanhood fibre.

Frank Crane

JULY 20

Morning: God is God. Because He is God, He is worthy of my trust and obedience. I will find rest nowhere but in His holy will, a will that is unspeakably beyond my largest notions of what He is up to.

Elisabeth Elliot

Evening: Regardless of how much patience we have, we would prefer never to use any of it.

James T. O'Brien

JULY 21

Morning: The will to win is important, but the will to prepare is vital.

Joe Paterno

Evening: Respect for ourselves guides our morals; respect for others guides our manners.

Laurence Sterne

JULY 22

Morning: Holding on to anger is like grasping a hot coal with the intent of throwing it at someone else; you are the one who gets burned.

Buddha

Evening: Reason and judgment are the qualities of a leader.

Tacitus

JULY 23

Morning: Procrastination is the art of keeping up with yesterday.

Don Marquis

Evening: The sun does not shine for a few trees and flowers, but for the wide world's joy.

Henry Ward Beecher

JULY 24

Morning: Love is an act of endless forgiveness.

Jean Vanier

Evening: He who cannot forgive breaks the bridge over which he himself must pass!

Scott Nicholson

JULY 25

Morning: The best remedy for those who are afraid, lonely or unhappy is to go outside, somewhere where they can be quiet, alone with the heavens, nature and God. Because only then does one feel that all is as it should be and that God wishes to see people happy, amidst the simple beauty of nature.

Anne Frank

Evening: Remember, what you say comes back to you.

Zig Ziglar

JULY 26

Morning: The tragedy of life and of the world is not that men do not know God; the tragedy is that, knowing Him, they still insist on going their own way.

William Barclay

Evening: The years teach much which the days never knew.

Ralph Waldo Emerson

JULY 27

Morning: My mother drew a distinction between achievement and success. She said that achievement is the knowledge that you have studied and worked hard and done the best that is in you. Success is being praised by others. That is nice but not as important or satisfying. Always aim for achievement and forget about success.

Helen Hayes

Evening: Love yourself and be awake—today, tomorrow, always.

Unknown

JULY 28

Morning: Responsibility is the price of freedom.

Elbert Hubbard

Evening: The way to succeed is to double your failure rate.

Thomas Watson

JULY 29

Morning: Your vision will become clear only when you look into your heart.

Carl Jung

Evening: It takes seventy-two muscles to frown, but only thirteen to smile.

Unknown

JULY 30

Morning: There is nothing that cannot be achieved by firm imagination.

Japanese Proverb

Evening: Obstacles don't have to stop you. If you run into a wall, don't turn around and give up. Figure out how to climb it, go through it, or work around it.

Michael Jordan

JULY 31

Morning: Persistence is to the character of man as carbon is to steel.

Napoleon Hill

Evening: Freedom is an internal achievement rather than an external adjustment.

Adam Clayton Powell

AUGUST 1

Morning: The future is not a gift—it is an achievement.

Harry Lauder

Evening: It is what we do easily and what we like to do that we do well.

Orison Swett Marden

AUGUST 2

Morning: One of the best rules in conversation is, never to say a thing which any of the company can reasonably wish had been left unsaid.

Jonathan Swift

Evening: There are no secrets to success. It is the result of preparation, hard work, learning from failure.

Colin Powell

AUGUST 3

Morning: The best years of your life are the ones in which you decide your problems are your own. You do not blame them on your mother, the ecology, or the president. You realize that you control your own destiny.

Albert Ellis

Evening: Am I not destroying my enemies when I make friends of them?

Abraham Lincoln

AUGUST 4

Morning: All right Mister, let me tell you what winning means. You're willing to go longer, work harder, give more than anyone else.
Vincent Lombardi

Evening: There are admirable potentialities in every human being. Believe in your strength and your truth. Learn to repeat endlessly to yourself, "It all depends on me."
Andre Gide

AUGUST 5

Morning: Opportunities are never lost; they are taken by others.
Unknown

Evening: He who has learned to pray has learned the greatest secret of a holy and happy life.
William Law

AUGUST 6

Morning: At the center of your being you have the answer; you know who you are and you know what you want.
Lao Tzu

Evening: When you discover your mission, you will feel its demand. It will fill you with enthusiasm and a burning desire to get to work on it.
W. Clement Stone

AUGUST 7

Morning: Above all be of single aim; have a legitimate and useful purpose, and devote yourself unreservedly to it.

James Allen

Evening: An aim in life is the only fortune worth finding.

Jacqueline Kennedy Onassis

AUGUST 8

Morning: Blessed are those who can give without remembering and take without forgetting.

Elizabeth Bibesco

Evening: It is usually the imagination that is wounded first, rather than the heart, it being much more sensitive.

Henry David Thoreau

AUGUST 9

Morning: When you say that a situation or a person is hopeless, you are slamming the door in the face of God.

Charles L. Allen

Evening: It is essential that we enable young people to see themselves as participants in one of the most exciting eras in history, and to have a sense of purpose in relation to it.

Nelson Rockefeller

AUGUST 10

Morning: We cannot change our past. We cannot change the fact that people act in a certain way. We cannot change the inevitable. The only thing we can do is play on the one string we have, and that is our attitude.

Charles R. Swindoll

Evening: Real success comes in small portions day by day. You need to take pleasure in life's daily little treasures. It is the most important thing in measuring success.

Denis Waitley

AUGUST 11

Morning: He who has a why to live for can bear almost any how.

Friedrich Nietzsche

Evening: Remember your yesterdays, dream your tomorrows, live your todays.

Unknown

AUGUST 12

Morning: The more you lose yourself in something bigger than yourself, the more energy you will have.

Norman Vincent Peale

Evening: Optimism is the faith that leads to achievement. Nothing can be done without hope or confidence.

Helen Keller

AUGUST 13

Morning: One must never lose time in vainly regretting the past nor in complaining about the changes which cause us discomfort, for change is the very essence of life.

Anatole France

Evening: One problem with gazing too frequently into the past is that we may turn around to find the future has run out on us.

Michael Cibenko

AUGUST 14

Morning: We are not here merely to make a living. We are here to enrich the world.

Woodrow Wilson

Evening: Minds are like parachutes—they only function when open.

Thomas Dewar

AUGUST 15

Morning: God has given each of us our "marching orders." Our purpose here on Earth is to find those orders and carry them out. Those orders acknowledge our special gifts.

Soren Kierkegaard

Evening: One of the virtues of being very young is that you don't let the facts get in the way of your imagination.

Sam Levenson

AUGUST 16

Morning: One of the lessons of history is that nothing is often a good thing to do and always a clever thing to say.

Will Durant

Evening: The people who get on in this world are the people who get up and look for the circumstances they want, and if they can't find them, make them.

George Bernard Shaw

AUGUST 17

Morning: The journey of a thousand miles starts with a single step.

Chinese Proverb

Evening: Remember, if you ever need a helping hand, you'll find one at the end of your arm. As you grow older you will discover that you have two hands. One for helping yourself, the other for helping others.

Audrey Hepburn

AUGUST 18

Morning: It doesn't matter if you try and try and try again, and fail. It does matter if you try and fail, and fail to try again.

Charles Kettering

Evening: Where there's life, there's hope.

Terence

AUGUST 19

Morning: I don't wait for moods. You accomplish nothing if you do that. Your mind must know it has got to get down to work.

Pearl S. Buck

Evening: Start by doing what's necessary; then do what's possible; and suddenly you are doing the impossible.

St. Francis of Assisi

AUGUST 20

Morning: Never waste a minute of your precious life by squandering it thinking about people you don't like.

Unknown

Evening: The supreme object of life is to live. Few people live. It is true life only to realize one's own perfection, to make one's every dream a reality.

Oscar Wilde

AUGUST 21

Morning: Mistakes are a fact of life. It is the response to error that counts.

Nikki Giovanni

Evening: Never let your head hang down. Never give up and sit down and grieve. Find another way.

Leroy "Satchel" Paige

AUGUST 22

Morning: Start every day with an inspiring thought.

Unknown

Evening: One may walk over the highest mountain one step at a time.

John Wanamaker

AUGUST 23

Morning: Love not what you are but what you may become.

Miguel De Cervantes

Evening: The distance is nothing; it's only the first step that is difficult.

Marquise du Deffand

AUGUST 24

Morning: I will! I am! I can! I will actualize my dream. I will press ahead. I will settle down and see it through. I will solve the problems. I will pay the price. I will never walk away from my dream until I see my dream walk away: Alert! Alive! Achieved!

Robert Schuller

Evening: Our wisdom comes from our experience, and our experience comes from our foolishness.

Sacha Guitry

AUGUST 25

Morning: Cherish your visions; cherish your ideals; cherish the music that stirs in your heart, the beauty that forms in your mind, the loveliness that drapes your purest thoughts, for out of them will grow delightful conditions, all heavenly environment; of these if you but remain true to them, your world will at last be built.

James Allen

Evening: I feel that the greatest reward for doing is the opportunity to do more.

Jonas Salk

AUGUST 26

Morning: Life, like all other games, becomes fun when one realizes that it's just a game.

Nerijus Stasiulis

Evening: Love is the great miracle cure. Loving ourselves works miracles in our lives.

Louise Hay

AUGUST 27

Morning: To be yourself in a world that is constantly trying to make you something else is the greatest accomplishment.

Ralph Waldo Emerson

Evening: To change and to change for the better are two different things.

German Proverb

AUGUST 28

Morning: Really think hard about what you want to do, because when you're doing what you want to do is probably when you'll be doing your best. And pray it is not a hobby, so they'll pay you for it.

Rush Limbaugh

Evening: Have courage for the great sorrows of life and patience for the small ones. And when you have finished your daily task, go to sleep in peace. God is awake.

Victor Hugo

AUGUST 29

Morning: You're never too old to become younger.

Mae West

Evening: The difference between the impossible and the possible lies in a person's determination.

Tommy Lasorda

AUGUST 30

Morning: Know yourself. Don't accept your dog's admiration as conclusive evidence that you are wonderful.

Ann Landers

Evening: Many of us spend half our time wishing for things we could have if we didn't spend half our time wishing.

Alexander Woollcott

AUGUST 31

Morning: In this world full of pain and sorrow, maybe once in a lifetime, you'll find someone who will make you feel wonderful. Hang on to that someone no matter what!

Unknown

Evening: Youth is a circumstance you can't do anything about. The trick is to grow up without getting old.

Frank Lloyd Wright

SEPTEMBER 1

Morning: If you see ten troubles coming down the road, you can be sure that nine will run into the ditch before they reach you.

Calvin Coolidge

Evening: God brings men into deep waters, not to drown them, but to cleanse them.

John H. Aughey

SEPTEMBER 2

Morning: Chance can allow you to accomplish a goal every once in a while, but consistent achievement happens only if you love what you are doing.

Bart Conner

Evening: An insincere and evil friend is more to be feared than a wild beast; a wild beast may wound your body, but an evil friend will wound your mind.

Buddha

SEPTEMBER 3

Morning: Life isn't about finding yourself. Life is about creating yourself.

George Bernard Shaw

Evening: Your own mind is a sacred enclosure into which nothing harmful can enter except by your permission.

Ralph Waldo Emerson

SEPTEMBER 4

Morning: Work is love made visible. And if you cannot work with love but only with distaste, it is better that you should leave your work and sit at the gate of the temple and take alms of those who work with joy.

Kahlil Gibran

Evening: Your net worth to the world is usually determined by what remains after your bad habits are subtracted from your good ones.

Benjamin Franklin

SEPTEMBER 5

Morning: I have missed more than 9,000 shots in my career. I have lost almost 300 games. On twenty-six occasions I have been entrusted to take the game-winning shot ... and missed. And I have failed over and over and over again in my life. And that is why ... I succeed.

Michael Jordan

Evening: A goal is a dream with a deadline.

Leo B. Helzel

SEPTEMBER 6

Morning: You cannot see faith, but you can see the footprints of the faithful. We must leave behind "faithful footprints" for others to follow.

Dennis Anderson

Evening: Snuggle in God's arms. When you are hurting, when you feel lonely, left out, let Him cradle you, comfort you, reassure you of His all-sufficient power and love.

Kay Arthur

SEPTEMBER 7

Morning: We ought not to be weary of doing little things for the love of God, who regards not the greatness of the work, but the love with which it is performed.

Brother Lawrence

Evening: Courage is what it takes to stand up and speak; courage is also what it takes to sit down and listen.

Winston Churchill

SEPTEMBER 8

Morning: Opportunity may knock only once, but temptation leans on the doorbell.

Unknown

Evening: Those who are lifting the world upward and onward are those who encourage more than criticize.

Elizabeth Harrison

SEPTEMBER 9

Morning: Not knowing when the dawn will come, I open every door.

Emily Dickinson

Evening: The jack of all trades seldom is good at any. Concentrate all of your efforts on one definite chief aim.

Napoleon Hill

SEPTEMBER 10

Morning: There is never time in the future in which we will work out our salvation. The challenge is in the moment; the time is always now.

James Baldwin

Evening: It takes both sunshine and rain to make a rainbow.

Unknown

SEPTEMBER 11

Morning: Salt, when dissolved in water, may disappear, but it does not cease to exist. We can be sure of its presence by tasting the water. Likewise, the indwelling Christ, though unseen, will be made evident to others from the love which he imparts to us.

Sadhu Sundar Singh

Evening: As long as you're going to think anyway, think big.

Donald Trump

SEPTEMBER 12

Morning: Life shrinks or expands in proportion to one's courage.

Anais Nin

Evening: Strange is our situation here upon earth. Each of us comes for a short visit, not knowing why, yet sometimes seeming to divine a purpose. From the standpoint of daily life, however, there is one thing we do know: that man is here for the sake of other men.

Albert Einstein

SEPTEMBER 13

Morning: Seek out that particular mental attribute which makes you feel most deeply and vitally alive, along with which comes the inner voice which says, "This is the real me," and when you have found that attitude, follow it.

William James

Evening: Don't pray when it rains if you don't pray when the sun shines.

Leroy "Satchel" Paige

SEPTEMBER 14

Morning: You miss 100 percent of the shots you never take.

Wayne Gretzky

Evening: The first teacher is our own heart.

Cheyenne Proverb

SEPTEMBER 15

Morning: Persuasion is better than force.

Unknown

Evening: It is a rough road that leads to the heights of greatness.

Seneca

SEPTEMBER 16

Morning: The life given us by nature is short, but the memory of a life well spent is eternal.

Marcus Tullius Cicero

Evening: Do not lose courage in considering your own imperfections but instantly set about remedying them—every day begin the task anew.

Francis de Sales

SEPTEMBER 17

Morning: When you come to a roadblock, take a detour.

Mary Kay Ash

Evening: I find the great thing in this world is not so much where we stand, as in what direction we are moving.

Oliver Wendell Holmes

SEPTEMBER 18

Morning: The greatest achievement was at first and for a time only a dream.

James Allen

Evening: The real power behind whatever success I have now was something I found within myself— something that's in all of us, I think, a little piece of God just waiting to be discovered.

Tina Turner

SEPTEMBER 19

Morning: My life is full of mistakes. They're like pebbles that make a good road.

Beatrice Wood

Evening: Who I have become is who I have always tried to be.

Samuel Jackson

SEPTEMBER 20

Morning: The two best times to plant a tree are twenty years ago and today.

Chinese Proverb

Evening: He is no fool who gives what he cannot keep to gain what he cannot lose.

Jim Elliot

SEPTEMBER 21

Morning: We don't always need to know where we are going as long as we know whom we are following. God is in control. Even when we wind up in strange places or unusual circumstances, the Father is not caught by surprise.

Mike Clay

Evening: It is never too late to become what you might have been.

George Eliot

SEPTEMBER 22

Morning: Life hasn't always smiled on me, but I have always smiled on life.

Raoul Dufy

Evening: What's ahead of me and what's behind me are nothing compared to what's inside me.

Jean Shapiro

SEPTEMBER 23

Morning: If I take care of my character, my reputation will take care of me.

Dwight L. Moody

Evening: Whatever you are, be a good one.

Abraham Lincoln

SEPTEMBER 24

Morning: Happiness is a butterfly which, when pursued, is always beyond your grasp, but which, if you will sit down quietly, may alight upon you.

Nathaniel Hawthorne

Evening: He who never made a mistake never made a discovery.

Unknown

SEPTEMBER 25

Morning: A man of genius makes no mistakes. His errors are volitional and are the portals of discovery.

James Joyce

Evening: One never notices what has been done; one can only see what remains to be done.

Marie Curie

SEPTEMBER 26

Morning: Winners take time to relish their work, knowing that scaling the mountain is what makes the view from the top so exhilarating.

Denis Waitley

Evening: Don't be afraid to give up the good to go for the great.

Kenny Rogers

SEPTEMBER 27

Morning: When we seek His word above all others, His encouragement before all others, His truth instead of all others, then we will be pleasing to Him more than all others.

Woodroll Kroll

Evening: Success does not come to those who wait, and it does not wait for anyone to come to it.

Unknown

SEPTEMBER 28

Morning: The moon is the first milestone on the road to the stars.

Arthur C. Clarke

Evening: The most effective way to do it, is to do it.

Toni Cade Bambara

SEPTEMBER 29

Morning: Imagination will often carry us to worlds that never were. But without it we go nowhere.

Carl Sagan

Evening: We live in the present, we dream of the future, and we learn eternal truths from the past.

Chiang Kai-Shek

SEPTEMBER 30

Morning: Each day provides its own gifts.
Martial

Evening: Every one of us lives his life just once; if we are honest, to live once is enough.
Greta Garbo

OCTOBER 1

Morning: Deserve your dream.
Octavio Paz

Evening: There are two kinds of failures: those who thought and never did, and those who did and never thought.
Laurence J. Peter

OCTOBER 2

Morning: Every single one of us can do things that no one else can do—can love things that no one else can love. We are like violins. We can be used for doorstops, or we can make music. You know what to do.
Barbara Sher

Evening: Success demands singleness of purpose.
Vincent Lombardi

OCTOBER 3

Morning: The greatest use of life is to spend it for something that outlasts it.

William James

Evening: Responsibilities gravitate to the person who can shoulder them.

Tom Stoppard

OCTOBER 4

Morning: Today, be aware of how you are spending your 1,440 beautiful moments, and spend them wisely.

Unknown

Evening: Imagination is the beginning of creation. You imagine what you desire, you will what you imagine, and at last you create what you will.

George Bernard Shaw

OCTOBER 5

Morning: Perseverance is failing nineteen times and succeeding the twentieth.

Julie Andrews

Evening: What makes life dreary is the want of a motive.

George Eliot

OCTOBER 6

Morning: Positive thinking is the key to success in business, education, pro football, anything that you can mention. I go out there thinking that I'm going to complete every pass.
Ron Jaworski

Evening: Find a purpose in life so big it will challenge every capacity to be at your best.
David O. McKay

OCTOBER 7

Morning: Achievement is not always success while reputed failure often is. It is honest endeavor, persistent effort to do the best possible under any and all circumstances.
Orison Swett Marden

Evening: The way to get started is to quit talking and begin doing.
Walt Disney

OCTOBER 8

Morning: Every calling is great when greatly pursued.
Oliver Wendell Holmes

Evening: Anyone can sympathize with the sufferings of a friend, but it requires a very fine nature to sympathize with a friend's success.
Oscar Wilde

OCTOBER 9

Morning: Look for an occupation that you like, and you will not need to labor for a single day in your life.

Confucius

Evening: When you cannot make up your mind which of two evenly balanced courses of action you should take—choose the bolder.

William Joseph Slim

OCTOBER 10

Morning: The biggest room in the world is the room for improvement.

Unknown

Evening: Life consists in what a man is thinking of all day.

Ralph Waldo Emerson

OCTOBER 11

Morning: All you have shall some day be given; therefore give now, that the season of giving may be yours and not your inheritors.

Kahlil Gibran

Evening: People are unreasonable, illogical, and self-centered. Love them anyway.

Bishop Abel Muzorewa

OCTOBER 12

Morning: Ability will never catch up with the demand for it.

Malcolm Forbes

Evening: High achievement always takes place in the framework of high expectation.

Jack Kinder

OCTOBER 13

Morning: I will permit no man to narrow and degrade my soul by making me hate him.

Booker T. Washington

Evening: If instead of a gem, or even a flower, we should cast the gift of a loving thought into the heart of a friend, that would be giving as the angels give.

George MacDonald

OCTOBER 14

Morning: We are the music makers, and we are the dreamers of dreams.

Arthur O'Shaughnessy

Evening: If there is light in the soul, there will be beauty in the person. If there is beauty in the person, there will be harmony in the house. If there is harmony in the house, there will be order in the nation. If there is order in the nation, there will be peace in the world.

Chinese Proverb

OCTOBER 15

Morning: Quite honestly, most people are quick to "write someone off." But our God is a God of the second chance. Learn from One who is patient with you, and you'll learn to be patient with others.

Woodroll Kroll

Evening: Dreams are renewable. No matter what our age or condition, there are still untapped possibilities within us and new beauty waiting to be born.

Dale E. Turner

OCTOBER 16

Morning: One out of four people in this country is mentally unbalanced. Think of your three closest friends; if they seem OK, then you're the one.

Ann Landers

Evening: Purpose serves as a principle around which to organize our lives.

Unknown

OCTOBER 17

Morning: Seek the wisdom of the ages, but look at the world through the eyes of a child.

Ron Wild

Evening: May you live all the days of your life.

Jonathan Swift

OCTOBER 18

Morning: Look at everything as though you were seeing it either for the first or last time. Then your time on earth will be filled with glory.
Betty Smith

Evening: The men who try to do something and fail are infinitely better than those who try to do nothing and succeed.
Lloyd Jones

OCTOBER 19

Morning: Nothing should be prized more highly than the value of each day.
Johann Wolfgang von Goethe

Evening: On days when life is difficult and I feel overwhelmed, as I do fairly often, it helps to remember in my prayers that all God requires of me is to trust Him and be His friend. I find I can do that.
Bruce Larson

OCTOBER 20

Morning: Life is not a "brief candle." It is a splendid torch that I want to make burn as brightly as possible before handing on to future generations.
George Bernard Shaw

Evening: God doesn't always smooth the path, but sometimes he puts springs in the wagon.
Marshall Lucas

OCTOBER 21

Morning: To have striven, to have made an effort, to have been true to certain ideals—this alone is worth the struggle. We are here to add what we can to, not to get what we can from, life.

Sir William Osler

Evening: We are more than what we do ... much more than what we accomplish ... far more than what we possess.

William Arthur Ward

OCTOBER 22

Morning: And forget not that the earth delights to feel your bare feet and the winds long to play with your hair.

Kahlil Gibran

Evening: Be such a man, and live such a life, that if every man were such as you, and every life a life like yours, this earth would be God's Paradise.

Phillips Brooks

OCTOBER 23

Morning: Work joyfully and peacefully, knowing that right thoughts and right efforts will inevitably bring about right results.

James Allen

Evening: Every blade of grass has its angel that bends over it and whispers, "Grow, grow."

The Talmud

OCTOBER 24

Morning: Be glad of life, because it gives you the chance to love and to work and to play and to look up at the stars.

Henry Van Dyke

Evening: All my life I've wanted to be somebody. But I see now I should have been more specific.

Jane Wagner

OCTOBER 25

Morning: People travel to wonder at the height of the mountains, at the huge waves of the seas, at the long course of the rivers, at the vast compass of the ocean, at the circular motion of the stars, and yet they pass by themselves without wondering.

St. Augustine

Evening: We are each of us angels with only one wing, and we can only fly by embracing one another.

Luciano de Crescenzo

OCTOBER 26

Morning: Did you never run for shelter in a storm, and find fruit which you expected not? Did you never go to God for safeguard, driven by outward storms, and there find unexpected fruit?

John Owen

Evening: Achieving starts with believing.

Unknown

OCTOBER 27

Morning: Service is the very purpose of life. It is the rent we pay for living on the planet.
Marian Wright Edelman

Evening: Never look down on anybody unless you're helping them up.
Jesse Jackson

OCTOBER 28

Morning: The question is not whether we will be extremists, but what kind of extremists we will be. ... The nation and the world are in dire need of creative extremists.
Martin Luther King, Jr.

Evening: Too many people today know the price of everything and the value of nothing.
Ann Landers

OCTOBER 29

Morning: The world has the habit of making room for the man whose words and actions show that he knows where he is going.
Napoleon Hill

Evening: It is not only for what we do that we are held responsible, but also for what we do not do.
Moliere

OCTOBER 30

Morning: It takes some of us a lifetime to learn that Christ, our Good Shepherd, knows exactly what He is doing with us. He understands us perfectly.

Phillip Keller

Evening: Every man is said to have his peculiar ambition.

Abraham Lincoln

OCTOBER 31

Morning: Self-reverence, self-knowledge, self-control—these three alone lead life to sovereign power.

Alfred, Lord Tennyson

Evening: Learn from the mistakes of others because you can't live long enough to make them all yourself.

Unknown

NOVEMBER 1

Morning: Strong lives are motivated by dynamic purposes; lesser ones exist on wishes and inclinations.

Kenneth Hildebrand

Evening: Kindness is in our power, even when fondness is not.

Samuel Johnson

NOVEMBER 2

Morning: Joy is but the sign that creative emotion is fulfilling its purpose.

Charles Du Bos

Evening: Jesus, like any good fisherman, first catches the fish; then He cleans them.

Mark Potter

NOVEMBER 3

Morning: Fame usually comes to those who are thinking about something else.

Oliver Wendell Holmes

Evening: Let us be grateful to people who make us happy; they are the charming gardeners who make our souls blossom.

Marcel Proust

NOVEMBER 4

Morning: The real contest is always between what you've done and what you're capable of doing. You measure yourself against yourself and nobody else.

Geoffrey Gaberino

Evening: We shall find peace. We shall hear angels. We shall see the sky sparkling with diamonds.

Anton Pavlovich Chekhov

NOVEMBER 5

Morning: Where others see but the dawn coming over the hill, I see the soul of God shouting for joy.

William Blake

Evening: Every noble work is at first impossible.

Thomas Carlyle

NOVEMBER 6

Morning: If you can imagine it, you can achieve it. If you can dream it, you can become it.

William Arthur Ward

Evening: Rich is the person who has a praying friend.

Janice Hughes

NOVEMBER 7

Morning: To aim at the best and to remain essentially ourselves is one and the same thing.

Janet Erskine Stuart

Evening: When tomorrow comes, this day will be gone forever; in its place is something that you have left behind. Let it be something good.

Unknown

NOVEMBER 8

Morning: Look at a day when you are supremely satisfied at the end. It's not a day when you lounge around doing nothing; it's when you've had everything to do, and you've done it.

Margaret Thatcher

Evening: Keep your feet on the ground and keep reaching for the stars.

Casey Kasem

NOVEMBER 9

Morning: Forever is composed of nows.

Emily Dickinson

Evening: If you don't change your beliefs, your life will be like this forever. Is that good news?

Robert Anthony

NOVEMBER 10

Morning: When we go fishing with Jesus for fish, we catch live ones, and they die! When we go fishing with Jesus for men, we catch dead ones, and they LIVE.

Unknown

Evening: One can never consent to creep when one feels an impulse to soar.

Helen Keller

NOVEMBER 11

Morning: If you fear making anyone mad, then you ultimately probe for the lowest common denominator of human achievement.

Jimmy Carter

Evening: The tallest trees are most in the power of the winds, and ambitious men of the blasts of fortune.

William Penn

NOVEMBER 12

Morning: Life is never easy for those who dream.

Robert James Waller

Evening: Ambition can creep as well as soar.

Edmund Burke

NOVEMBER 13

Morning: And the longer you delay, the more your sin gets strength and rooting. If you cannot bend a twig, how will you be able to bend it when it is a tree?

Richard Baxter

Evening: What the mind can conceive and believe, the mind can achieve.

Napoleon Hill

NOVEMBER 14

Morning: Death is not the greatest loss in life. The greatest loss is what dies inside us while we live.

Norman Cousins

Evening: Ambition is so powerful a passion in the human breast, that however high we reach we are never satisfied.

Niccolo Machiavelli

NOVEMBER 15

Morning: Use your precious moments to live life fully every single second of every single day.

Marcia Wieder

Evening: The good you do today will be forgotten tomorrow. Do good anyway.

Bishop Abel Muzorewa

NOVEMBER 16

Morning: You can observe a lot by just looking around.

Yogi Berra

Evening: Faith in a prayer-hearing God will make a prayer-loving Christian.

Andrew Murray

NOVEMBER 17

Morning: It's a good thing to have all the props pulled out from under us occasionally. It gives us some sense of what is rock under our feet, and what is sand.

Madeleine L'Engle

Evening: Blessed are the hearts that can bend; they shall never be broken.

Albert Camus

NOVEMBER 18

Morning: All things grow with time—except grief.

Unknown

Evening: Prayer is the spirit speaking truth to Truth.

Philip James Bailey

NOVEMBER 19

Morning: Chase your passion, not your pension.

Denis Waitley

Evening: Those who live in harmony with themselves live in harmony with the universe.

Marcus Aurelius Antoninus

NOVEMBER 20

Morning: Flatter me, and I may not believe you. Criticize me, and I may not like you. Ignore me, and I may not forgive you. Encourage me, and I may not forget you.

William Arthur

Evening: Nature does nothing uselessly.

Aristotle

NOVEMBER 21

Morning: If I were asked to give what I consider the single most useful bit of advice for all humanity it would be this: Expect trouble as an inevitable part of life, and when it comes, hold you head high, look it squarely in the eye, and say, "I will be bigger than you. You cannot defeat me."

Ann Landers

Evening: The important thing in life is not the triumph but the struggle.

Pierre de Coubertin

NOVEMBER 22

Morning: The reason why worry kills more people than work is that more people worry than work.

Robert Frost

Evening: My great concern is not whether you have failed, but whether you are content with your failure.

Abraham Lincoln

NOVEMBER 23

Morning: People do not attract that which they want, but that which they are.

James Allen

Evening: If you reach for the stars, you'll never wind up with a handful of mud.

Unknown

NOVEMBER 24

Morning: The mark of our ignorance is the depth of our belief in injustice and tragedy.

Richard Bach

Evening: If you have the will to win, you have achieved half your success; if you don't, you have achieved half your failure.

David V. A. Ambrose

NOVEMBER 25

Morning: I want to be thoroughly used up when I die, for the harder I work the more I live. I rejoice in life for its own sake.

George Bernard Shaw

Evening: Right is right, even if everyone is against it; and wrong is wrong, even if everyone is for it.

William Penn

NOVEMBER 26

Morning: If you think you can do it, you can. If you believe you can do it, you will. If you trust you can do it, you will make a difference.

Catherine Ellis

Evening: It is impossible for a man to be freed from the habit of sin before he hates it, just as it is impossible to receive forgiveness before confessing his trespasses.

Ignatius

NOVEMBER 27

Morning: A wise man sees as much as he ought, not as much as he can.

Montaigne

Evening: It is a shameful thing for the soul to faint while the body still perseveres.

Marcus Aurelius Antoninus

NOVEMBER 28

Morning: Failure is the condiment that gives success its flavor.

Truman Capote

Evening: Everybody is ignorant, only on different subjects.

Will Rogers

NOVEMBER 29

Morning: When inspiration does not come to me, I go halfway to meet it.

Sigmund Freud

Evening: The greatest feats of love are performed by those who have had much practice in performing daily acts of kindness.

Unknown

NOVEMBER 30

Morning: Cushion the painful effects of hard blows by keeping the enthusiasm going strong, even if doing so requires struggle.

Norman Vincent Peale

Evening: The best thing about the future is that it comes only one day at a time.

Abraham Lincoln

DECEMBER 1

Morning: When we long for life without difficulties, remind us that oaks grow strong in contrary winds and diamonds are made under pressure.

Peter Marshall

Evening: There's no substitute for hard work.

Thomas Edison

DECEMBER 2

Morning: Tell me what you like, and I'll tell you what you are.

John Ruskin

Evening: Time is free, but it's priceless. You can't own it, but you can use it. You can't keep it, but you can send it. Once you've lost it, you can never get it back.

Harvey Mackay

DECEMBER 3

Morning: We don't remember days; we remember moments.

Cesare Pavese

Evening: How can we be strangers, if we both follow Christ?

Unknown

DECEMBER 4

Morning: Singleness of purpose is one of the chief essentials for success in life, no matter what may be one's aim.

John D. Rockefeller

Evening: There are two educations. One should teach us how to make a living and the other how to live.

John Adams

DECEMBER 5

Morning: One who desires to excel should endeavor in those things that are in themselves most excellent.

Epictetus

Evening: You must have an aim, a vision, a goal. For the man sailing through life with no destination or port-of-call, every wind is the wrong wind.

Tracy Brinkmann

DECEMBER 6

Morning: As we trust God to give us wisdom for today's decisions, He will lead us a step at a time into what He wants us to be doing in the future.

Theodore Epp

Evening: Believe and act as if it were impossible to fail.

Charles Kettering

DECEMBER 7

Morning: In youth we learn; in age we understand.

Marie Von Ebner-Eschenbach

Evening: There are no menial jobs, only menial attitudes.

William John Bennett

DECEMBER 8

Morning: Attitudes are contagious. Is yours worth catching?

Unknown

Evening: Most people would succeed in small things if they were not troubled with great ambitions.

Henry Wadsworth Longfellow

DECEMBER 9

Morning: We succeed only as we identify in life, or in war, or in anything else, a single overriding objective, and make all other considerations bend to that one objective.

Dwight D. Eisenhower

Evening: You must begin to think of yourself as becoming the person you want to be.

David Viscott

DECEMBER 10

Morning: It is not how much we have, but how much we enjoy, that makes happiness.

Charles Haddon Spurgeon

Evening: You may be disappointed if you fail, but you are doomed if you don't try.

Beverly Sills

DECEMBER 11

Morning: Outstanding people have one thing in common: an absolute sense of mission.

Zig Ziglar

Evening: Each of us may be sure that if God sends us on stony paths, He will provide us with strong shoes, and He will not send us out on any journey for which He does not equip us well.

Alexander MacLaren

DECEMBER 12

Morning: Too many people grow up. That's the real trouble with the world: too many people grow up. They forget. They don't remember what it's like to be twelve years old. They patronize; they treat children as inferiors. Well, I won't do that.

Walt Disney

Evening: The education of the will is the object of our existence.

Ralph Waldo Emerson

DECEMBER 13

Morning: What you keep to yourself, you lose; what you give away, you keep forever.

Axel Munthe

Evening: There is nothing permanent except change.

Heraclitus

DECEMBER 14

Morning: There is no elevator to success. You have to take the stairs.

Unknown

Evening: There is no sadder sight than a young pessimist.

Mark Twain

DECEMBER 15

Morning: We have a choice. We can carry the world on our shoulders, or we can say, "I give up, Lord; here's my life. I give you my world, the whole world."

Bruce Larson

Evening: If we put off repentance another day, we have a day more to repent of, and a day less to repent in.

Mason

DECEMBER 16

Morning: The miracle is not to fly in the air, or to walk on the water, but to walk on the earth.

Chinese Proverb

Evening: The greatest and most important problems in life are all in a certain sense insoluble. They can never be solved, but only outgrown.

Carl Jung

DECEMBER 17

Morning: All of us have at least one great voice deep inside.

Pat Riley

Evening: Be yourself. The world worships the original.

Ingrid Bergman

DECEMBER 18

Morning: To live is so startling it leaves little time for anything else.

Emily Dickinson

Evening: We are shaped and fashioned by what we love.

Johann Wolfgang von Goethe

DECEMBER 19

Morning: There are many of us who are willing to do great things for the Lord, but few of us are willing to do little things.

Dwight L. Moody

Evening: You can only be young once. But you can always be immature.

Dave Barry

DECEMBER 20

Morning: Promise yourself to live in faith that the whole world is on your side so long as you are true to the best that is in you.

Christian Larson

Evening: Failure is the path of least persistence.

Unknown

DECEMBER 21

Morning: It is time to break through the barriers that have held you back and held you down for such a long time. It is time to reach out and indelibly etch your place in history.

Greg Hickman

Evening: Let us endeavor to live so that when we come to die, even the undertaker will be sorry.

Mark Twain

DECEMBER 22

Morning: Happiness comes when we test our skills toward some meaningful purpose.

John Stossel

Evening: Nobody ever drowned in his own sweat.

Ann Landers

DECEMBER 23

Morning: Wisdom is, and starts with, the humility to accept the fact that you don't have all the right answers, and the courage to learn to ask the right questions.

Unknown

Evening: Virtue is not left to stand alone. He who practices it will have neighbors.

Confucius

DECEMBER 24

Morning: Never mistake activity for achievement.

John Wooden

Evening: When you wholeheartedly adopt a "with all your heart" attitude and go out with the positive principle, you can do incredible things.

Norman Vincent Peale

DECEMBER 25

Morning: Enthusiasm, if fueled by inspiration and perseverance, travels with passion, and its destination is excellence.

Napoleon Hill

Evening: The great use of life is to spend it on something that will outlast it.

William James

DECEMBER 26

Morning: Don't accept that others know you better than yourself. Work joyfully and peacefully, knowing that right thoughts and right efforts will inevitably bring about right results.

James Allen

Evening: I've got a great ambition to die of exhaustion rather than boredom.

Angus Grossart

DECEMBER 27

Morning: When it's all over, it's not who you were. It's whether you made a difference.

Unknown

Evening: Associate yourself with men of good quality if you esteem your own reputation, for 'tis better to be alone than in bad company.

George Washington

DECEMBER 28

Morning: Never let a problem to be solved become more important than a person to be loved.

Barbara Johnson

Evening: The influence of each human being on others in this life is a kind of immortality.

John Quincy Adams

DECEMBER 29

Morning: Life's tragedy is that we get old too soon and wise too late.

Benjamin Franklin

Evening: As we grow better, we meet better people.

Elbert Hubbard

DECEMBER 30

Morning: Only when your consciousness is totally focused on the moment you are in can you receive whatever gift, lesson, or delight that moment has to offer.

Barbara De Angelis

Evening: The love of our neighbor in all its fullness simply means being able to say to him, "What are you going through?"

Simone Weil

DECEMBER 31

Morning: These then are my last words to you: Be not afraid of life. Believe that life is worth living and your belief will help create the fact.

William James

Evening: I know the power obedience has of making things easy which seem impossible.

Teresa of Avila

NOTES